Watergate: The Scandal That Brought Down a President

By Charles River Editors

President Nixon shortly before leaving the White House on August 9, 1974

About Charles River Editors

Charles River Editors was founded by Harvard and MIT alumni to provide superior editing and original writing services, with the expertise to create digital content for publishers across a vast range of subject matter. In addition to providing original digital content for third party publishers, Charles River Editors republishes civilization's greatest literary works, bringing them to a new generation via ebooks.

Introduction

President Nixon leaving the White House on August 9, 1974.

Watergate

"I have never been a quitter. To leave office before my term is completed is abhorrent to every instinct in my body. But as President, I must put the interest of America first. America needs a full-time President and a full-time Congress, particularly at this time with problems we face at home and abroad. To continue to fight through the months ahead for my personal vindication would almost totally absorb the time and attention of both the President and the Congress in a period when our entire focus should be on the great issues of peace abroad and prosperity without inflation at home. Therefore, I shall resign the Presidency effective at noon tomorrow. Vice President Ford will be sworn in as President at that hour in this office." – President Richard Nixon, August 8, 1974.

Increasingly and mistakenly viewed as a single scandal within the United States government, what is commonly referred to as the Watergate scandal serves as an overarching term for a series of scandals beginning in 1971 and extending through 1974, although more than any other, it refers to the specific break-in at the Watergate Hotel and office complex in Washington, D.C. The crisis, originating in a secretive battle between the two major political parties, the Nixon White House's paranoia, and the ensuing conflict concerning the release of confidential information to the public, induced senior government officials into committing crimes (most notoriously petty burglary) and coverups for the purposes of character assassination and inter-political espionage, and it ultimately resulted in the first and only resignation of a sitting American president, Richard Milhous Nixon. Watergate has since become so synonymous with scandal that "gate" is typically added to the end of words associated with scandals even today, and the Watergate complex still remains well known ("Even today, it is home to former Senator Bob Dole, and was the place where Monica Lewinsky laid low.")[1]

In the wake of the seemingly peculiar burglary, gradual media and judicial pursuits of the thread of scandals led from one thing to another over the following years until it began to culminate with Congressional impeachment proceedings and a momentous showdown between the President and the Supreme Court over the release of presidential tapes, a moment in which Nixon seriously considered defying the Court and initiating a constitutional crisis. When he at last surrendered them, excerpts were blatantly missing, most famously an 18 minute stretch. Given the flurry of activities, it has only been in recent years that historians have gained a full measure of the nation's perilous status during the intense battle between the various branches of the federal government, and the American public's view of government in general took a decidedly negative turn, resulting in social and political disillusionment and distrust of the government that still resonates today. If anything good came out of the Watergate scandal, it was that "in its wake, Watergate spawned a reform-minded Congress."[2]

For the last 40 years, President Nixon has been mostly reviled, and understandably, he's ranked among the country's worst presidents, but this view of the President and the Watergate scandal was not and still is not necessarily unanimous. A growing number of Republicans, led by conservatives such as former Nixon speechwriter Pat Buchanan, describe the bringing down of the president as a quasi-coup generated by the press and liberal social forces from within the anti-war movement, which gravitated to the release of information on Vietnam, an increasingly unpopular war, and tapping the widespread campus unrest throughout the country. Paul Johnson, in his book, *Modern Times: A History of the World from the 1920s to the Year 2000*, referred to the whole affair as nothing more than "this Watergate witch hunt." [3]

Watergate: The Scandal That Brought Down a President chronicles the controversial events that led to Nixon's resignation and the impact the scandal has had on American politics ever

---

[1] Watergate.info - Watergate: "The Scandal that Brought Down Richard Nixon" - www.watergate.info
[2] Mary Ferrell Foundation - Watergate - www.maryferrell.org
[3] Paul Johnson, "Modern Times: A History of the World from the 1920s to the Year 2000", Harper Collins: 2006

since. Along with pictures of important people, places, and events, you will learn about Watergate like you never have before, in no time at all.

Chapter 1: The Pentagon Papers, CREEP, and the First Burglaries

"The main further question is the extent to which we should add elements to the above actions that would tend deliberately to provoke a [North Vietnamese] reaction, and consequent retaliation by us.

Examples of actions to be considered would be running US naval patrols increasingly close to the North Vietnamese coast and/or associating them with 34A operations.

We believe such deliberately provocative elements should not be added in the immediate future while the GVN is still struggling to its feet. By early October, however, we may recommend such actions depending on [South Vietnam's] progress and Communist reaction in the meantime, especially to US naval patrols.." – The Pentagon Papers

Mistrust of government was certainly not a new phenomenon when Richard Nixon won the election of 1968 against an opposing Congress for the first time in over a century, but a new culture of secrecy and retaliation would further sour the public's perception of national leadership in the long-term. The psyche of the Nixon White House, as it has come to be better understood, was intricate and calculating. On the night of the 1968 victory celebration, Nixon was said to be "clouded by his reference to the problems of an unsettled war in Vietnam." And yet, it is said that he had scuttled South Vietnam's final hours at the Paris Peace Talks in an effort to stall the resolution until he could be elected. Speaking with the South Vietnamese, and allegedly promising a better deal than they would receive from Humphrey, the delegation vacated the negotiating table until after the election.

Nixon

The generally accepted profile of Nixon today is built largely upon Watergate, but such was not the case in the early 1970s. That said, a quiet movement among writers and biographers hinted at the trouble to come. Three psycho-biographies suggest that Nixon exhibited "dangerous personality characteristics" in George Reedy's *The Twilight of the Presidency*, Arthur Schlesinger's *The Imperial Presidency* and *The Politics of Lying: Government Deception, Secrecy and Power of David Wise*. With an increasing appetite for surveillance and the use of federal agencies to monitor and influence enemies, Nixon has been described as "a secretive man who did not tolerate criticism well, engaged in numerous acts of duplicity, who kept lists of enemies, and who used the power of the presidency to seek petty acts of revenge on those enemies." [4]

Although Watergate is named after the complex that housed the Democratic National Committee in 1972, and the attempted burglary of the DNC offices is often considered the first incident leading to the scandal, but Watergate truly had its roots in Daniel Ellsberg's leak of the Pentagon Papers to the *New York Times* in 1971. The Pentagon Papers outlined the course of American intervention in Vietnam, and that summer, the *New York Times* released a series of articles about the papers under the headline "Vietnam Archive: Pentagon Study Traces Three

---

[4] Watergate Scandal Timeline - www. authentichistory.com

Decades of Growing U.S. Involvement". Coming near the height of the Vietnam War's unpopularity, the leak of the Pentagon Papers badly damaged public morale, and the Nixon Administration sought an injunction to prevent the *Times* from disclosing the previously confidential information. When the *Times* appealed that injunction, it led to *New York Times Co. v. United States*, a suit that quickly reached the Supreme Court.

Ellsberg

Meanwhile, Ellsberg also disclosed information from the Pentagon Papers to the Washington Post, which also began to run stories, and this time, a federal judge refused the request for an injunction, writing, "The security of the Nation is not at the ramparts alone. Security also lies in the value of our free institutions. A cantankerous press, an obstinate press, an ubiquitous press must be suffered by those in authority in order to preserve the even greater values of freedom of expression and the right of the people to know." The government's appeal of that decision led to that case being brought before the Supreme Court along with the *New York Times* case. On June 30, 1971, the Supreme Court ruled in favor of the papers, holding that the government failed to meet its burden of proof for upholding an injunction against the release of the information.

Although the Pentagon Papers mostly covered the Kennedy and Johnson Administration, they were deemed embarrassing enough for the Nixon Administration, as asserted on one tape by Nixon's chief of staff, H.R. Haldeman: "[Donald] Rumsfeld was making this point this morning... To the ordinary guy, all this is a bunch of gobbledygook. But out of the gobbledygook comes a very clear thing.... It shows that people do things the president wants to do even though it's wrong, and the president can be wrong." Nixon's bent for secrecy was brought to full flower by Ellsberg's leaks of classified materials on the Vietnam War, especially when the federal government unsuccessfully fought Ellsberg on every front to prevent or diminish the impact of the Pentagon Papers' publication. In the wake of the Supreme Court decision, the Nixon Administration aimed to punish Ellsberg for what the president saw as an act of treason, and this led to the first noteworthy White House related burglary: an attempt to obtain damaging personal material against Ellsberg in the office of his Washington psychiatrist.

Haldeman

The Nixon administration's response to what it saw as a clear case of treason was to dub such forces as "counter-government," particularly those who supported the publication of the Pentagon Papers in the *New York Times*. As such, the Administration decided to counter Ellsberg and future leaks by forming a "special investigations unit," which would come to be known in time as the "plumbers." The principal figures of this unit included John Ehrlichman, John Paisley (liaison to the CIA), and E. Howard Hunt, a former top-level CIA agent.

At the head of the operation was Nixon's own chief of staff, Haldeman, who served as both recruiter and gatekeeper, once describing himself as "the president's son-of-a-bitch." The entire operation was carried out under the umbrella of the Committee to Re-elect the President, which would later be derisively referred to as CREEP. Gordon Liddy, who would become one of the most high-profile figures in the operation, was recruited by White House Counsel John Dean as a general intelligence gatherer. The crux of the unit's activities was to "harass Nixon's opponents...with wiretaps, burglaries and intercepted mail." The FBI was discouraged from getting near the incident through the White House suggestion that the break-in was a national security operation executed by the CIA.

Hunt

Ehrlichman

Dean, a precocious 32 year old Georgetown graduate, was appointed to White House Counsel after early reviews from his employer raving about his intelligence and skill. "As Watergate broke...[he was] to control the fall out after the burglars were arrested, which involved paying them large sums of money." Dean handled it well, and Nixon applauded, noting to Haldeman that the young lawyer was "a pretty good gem."[5]

According to the White House tapes, Nixon authorized a smear campaign against Ellsberg in July 1971. With that, an agenda of harassments began against Nixon opponents, and though several were canceled before they were attempted, the most noteworthy was not. Hunt personally investigated Ted Kennedy's Chappaquiddick scandal and any potential Kennedy involvement in the assassination of South Vietnamese leader Ngo Dinh Diem, but before the Watergate burglary, the plumbers' most important activity was the September 1971 burglary of Ellsberg's psychiatrist's office. The office's files were ransacked in an attempt for the Nixon Administration to obtain confidential information on Ellsberg, but the burglary, described in Ehrlichman's notes as "Hunt/Liddy Special Project No. 1", failed to turn up Ellsberg's files. Hunt and Liddy then suggested breaking into Ellsberg's psychiatrist's home, but that attempt was never made after Ehrlichman shot it down.

In taking these measures, Nixon's strategy relied on past experience, notably his prosecution of Alger Hiss in 1950. Nixon intended to try Ellsberg through the press, believing that the Justice Department would not follow through, and he boasted on the notorious presidential tapes of the

---

[5] NBClearn - John Dean Testifies Before Watergate Committee - www.nbclearn.com/portal/site/k-12/flatview?cuecard=72

leaks he had initiated in the earlier Hiss case. Just as the Justice Department dragged its feet in 1950 (at least according to Nixon), the same was true of the FBI in 1971, because Director J. Edgar Hoover refused to authorize an investigation of Ellsberg. As the *Washington Post*'s famous confidential source, "Deep Throat", later explained, "The problem was that the FBI wouldn't burglarize."

Though it wouldn't be revealed for several decades, Deep Throat was Deputy Director of the FBI Mark Felt. As second-in-command at the FBI, Felt had come to Washington to work in the offices of Senator Pope from Idaho, and as a graduate of the George Washington Law School, he held positions at the Federal Trade Commission and other agencies as well. Trained in espionage at the Academy in Quantico, he spent time in the West dealing with organized crime. As a high-ranking member of the FBI, and following the Death of J. Edgar Hoover, Felt had access to literally every scrap of material on the Watergate affair. As Deep Throat, he funneled a constant flow of information and confirmed certain suspicions to the *Washington Post*, and Nixon himself even suspected Felt, saying on tape that he was most likely an informer. As Woodward recalled, "The FBI was battling for its independence against the Nixon administration. Felt was a dashing gray-haired figure...and his experience as an anti-Nazi spy hunter...endowed him with a whole bag of counterintelligence tricks."

Felt

Felt's role as Deep Throat also came about in part due to Nixon's campaign against Ellsberg. With the administration attempting to pull in the FBI as a tool of the presidency rather than as an independently functioning investigative body, a natural resentment added to Felt's circumstantial motivation to assume the role he did. By drawing the FBI closer under his own direction, Nixon was trying to alter the body that would ordinarily investigate the federal government into a weapon with which to harass and illegally investigate others. Felt took this to heart as deeply as anyone in the Bureau, and "was so wounded that he was passed over for the top job, furious at Nixon's choice of an outsider...and determined that the White House not be allowed to steer and stall the Bureau's Watergate investigation, [that he] slipped into the role that would forever alter his life."[6]

While the burglary of Ellsberg's psychiatrist's office went through (albeit unsuccessfully), several operations were halted in mid-planning due to their high risk nature. On June 7, 1972, Nixon ordered the burglary of the Brookings Institute, a Washington think-tank, and in the order was his clearly expressed sentiment: "I want the Brookings safe cleared out." He further recommended that Haldeman speak with E. Howard Hunt, described by Haldeman as "ruthless, quiet, careful - kind of a tiger. He spent 20 years in the CIA overthrowing governments." [7] The intended burglary of the Brookings Institute was neither the first nor the gentlest plan to be drawn up; Charles Colson, considered the "evil genius" of the White House staff, initially recommended that the Brookings be firebombed. Ultimately, no attempt was never made.

Meanwhile, the intent to break-into the editor's office of the *Las Vegas Sun* was based on its relationship with billionaire Howard Hughes, whose associate, Robert Meheu, possessed damaging evidence against Democratic presidential candidate Edmund Muskie. This "mission" was halted as well; a general point of strategy, introduced by Gordon Liddy, was voted down by the White House Staff, with John Dean observing that such things should not be discussed within the Office of the Attorney General. The subject matter even included the formation of a prostitution ring in Washington to be used for intelligence gathering.

---

[6] David von Drehle, Washington Post Politics
[7] History Commons, Watergate - *The White House Plumbers*

Liddy in 1964

John Dean in 1972

On July 7, 1972, E. Howard Hunt was appointed to the White House staff, an appointment that represented a ratcheting up of the hardball style. At the time of Hunt's appointment, Nixon is quoted as saying, "Whoever opposes us, we will destroy. As a matter of fact, anyone who doesn't support us, we will destroy."

Ultimately, Ellsberg would be tried under the Espionage Act of 1917 for the disclosures, but fittingly, the case led to revelations of illegal wiretapping and the attempted burglary of his psychiatrist's office that compelled the judge to dismiss the case against Ellsberg in early May 1973: "The totality of the circumstances of this case which I have only briefly sketched offend a sense of justice. The bizarre events have incurably infected the prosecution of this case." Less than two weeks earlier, those same revelations would force the resignations of Ehrlichman, Haldeman, Dean, and U.S. Attorney General Richard Kleindienst on April 30. Looking back at it all, Ellsberg would later proclaim, "The public is lied to every day by the President, by his spokespeople, by his officers. If you can't handle the thought that the President lies to the public for all kinds of reasons, you couldn't stay in the government at that level, or you're made aware of it, a week. ... The fact is Presidents rarely say the whole truth—essentially, never say the whole truth—of what they expect and what they're doing and what they believe and why they're doing it and rarely refrain from lying, actually, about these matters."

Chapter 2: The Watergate Break-Ins

The Watergate complex

While the attempted burglaries related to Ellsberg would go unnoticed for several months, the break-ins related to the Watergate complex would not. Hunt would later testify that the initial decision to break-into Watergate was because Liddy had received information that "the Cuban government was supplying funds to the Democratic Party", and to "investigate this report, a surreptitious entry of Democratic national headquarters at the Watergate was made."

Although records recently unsealed seem to support Hunt's testimony, Liddy contradicted it, claiming he had received an order from Nixon aide Jeb Magruder to break-in because the Administration "wanted to hear anything that was going on inside the office of Larry O'Brien, who was the chairman of the DNC". Magruder further told Liddy he "wanted to be able to monitor his telephone conversations."

Magruder

As it turned out, Liddy had already considered breaking into Watergate, in an effort to target "the DNC headquarters for later, when and if it became the headquarters of the successful Democratic candidate at their convention". Liddy also recalled telling Magruder he could successfully break-in: "Yes. It's a high-security building, but we can do it." However, due to lack of surviving evidence, it's unclear exactly when Nixon Administration officials first discussed breaking into Watergate, and it's also unclear how many previous break-ins took place before the most famous one. Hunt later seemed confused about the nature of previous attempts in May 1973 when he testified: "I recall something about that, but it seems to me that was more in the nature of a familiarization tour, that McCord took not more than one or two of the men up there and walked them down to the sixth floor to show them the actual door. Then they simply got back into the elevator. It was simply a familiarizing with the operational problem of the two glass doors that opened into the Democratic National headquarters."

However, James McCord's version of events is crucially different. An electronics specialist, he was recruited specifically for such work in order to bug the phone of Democratic Chairman Larry O'Brien and that of R. Spencer Oliver, the Executive Director of the Association of State Democratic Chairmen. The first break-in attempts in May were successful, and Alfred Baldwin, look-out for the operation, would monitor over 200 calls over the next 20 days. McCord soon realized, however, that one of the bugs wasn't working and had to be replaced. In addition to the need for information that could be gained, news had reached him that the Veterans Against the Vietnam War had opened a desk at the Democratic National Committee. McCord argued "that it was worth going in [again] to see what they could discover about the anti-war activists."

McCord

The break-in at the Watergate Hotel on June 17, 1972 was actually a follow-up mission from a previous break-in several weeks prior to repair dysfunctional spy-taps and to photograph further files. However, on this break-in, the simple existence of a piece of tape over a door lock proved to be the origin of the Administration's fall. The tape was noticed by security guard Frank Willis, in charge of patrolling the luxury apartments and offices of the Watergate, and during his first pass of the evening, Willis removed the tape, assuming it had been placed there by one of the maintenance crews. On his second pass, he saw that the tape had been replaced and realized that something was amiss, so he called the Washington, D.C. police.

That evening, five men were arrested for breaking into the headquarters of the Democratic National Committee: Bernard Barker, Virgilio Gonzalez, Eugenio Martinez, James McCord Jr., and Frank Sturgis. The arrest would have remained a completely non-noteworthy case of break-in had not James McCord been carrying in his notebook the telephone number of E. Howard Hunt, thereby linking the crime to a White House staff member close to the president. Furthermore, $100 bills in possession of the five were traced by sequential serial numbers and were easily traced to a bank account of Barker, then to CREEP. Working under the Committee to Re-elect the President (later called CREEP), a fund-raising organization, those arrested represented a membership that included (a) Kenneth Dahlberg, Midwest Finance Chairman, (b) E. Howard Hunt, former agent for the CIA, and now only designated as a "campaign member," (c) Fred LaRue, Campaign Political Operative, (d) G. Gordon Liddy (campaign member) (e) Jeb Stuart Magruder, Campaign Manager, (f) James W. McCord, Campaign Security Coordinator (g) John Mitchell, Campaign Director, (h) Donald Segretti, Campaign Political Operative and (i) Hugh Sloan, Campaign Treasurer. It was Segretti who was predominantly in charge of the various break-ins ordered by CREEP, including an FBI investigation of CBS reporter Daniel Schorr, while Gordon Liddy was behind a largely unformulated plan to assassinate columnist Jack Anderson.

Shortly after the capture, a listening post was discovered at the Howard Johnson across the street from the Watergate, and the look-out man, Alfred Baldwin, was found first. Apparently, Liddy and Hunt were stationed there to remain in communication throughout the operation, and given that several of the conspirators were former agents in the CIA, suspicion immediately grew about just how "former" they really were. Barker's codename was AMCLATTER-1 in CIA files, and he had been a paid agent since 1966. Gonzalez was a former agent, and Martinez was a current agent. Hunt, the most high-level agent of all, could not be officially pinned down, listed in CREEP as only a "member." In all, over half a million dollars would be spent by CREEP in lawyer fees alone in the trials of these five, and the linking of lawyer fees to the administration provided the second spark that moved the Watergate story forward.

Chapter 3: The Administration's Initial Coverup Attempts

"A third rate burglary attempt." – Ron Ziegler, White House Press Secretary

Bob Woodward was present at the five arraignments "and overheard McCord mention CIA in connection with his occupation."[8] It was this revelation that compelled him to continue investigating, and as he was beginning his initial work, the coverup of the burglary attempt was

---

[8] U.S. History.com - Watergate Scandal - www.u-s-history.com/page/h1791.html

already underway. It seems Nixon was unaware of the activities that led to the Watergate break-in, and in a meeting on June 23, Nixon asked Haldeman, "Who was the asshole who ordered it?" However, the inclusion of Hunt's name forced the Administration to scramble immediately after the arrests took place. Dean claimed Ehrlichman ordered him to destroy records related to Hunt, and though Ehrlichman denied that, the evidence was ultimately destroyed by the White House Counsel and the FBI's Acting Director, L. Patrick Gray. "Magruder and others destroyed documents and lied to investigators."[9] Nixon also instructed Haldeman to obstruct the FBI investigation when he realized that John Mitchell, head of CREEP, was involved. Mitchell immediately resigned for "personal reasons."

In McCord's view, the president took matters in a fateful direction following the arrests by attempting to disguise the break-in as a CIA operation, which could not possibly hold up without the CIA falsely backing up his story. While Nixon might have believed that possible, McCord believed the right people were not in place for that to occur, and sensing what was about to happen, McCord wrote a hurried letter to Jack Caulfield, the Assistant Director of Crime Enforcement, telling him that if "[CIA Director Richard] Helms goes, and if the operation is laid at the CIA's feet, where it does not belong, every tree in the forest will fall. It will be a scorched desert." Nevertheless, Nixon went to Helms in an attempt to force the CIA to pay hush money for the five arrestees at the Watergate, and while others at the agency were willing to go along with that, Helms flatly refused. Helms later pointed out that the CIA " could get the money. ... We didn't need to launder money…[but] the end result would have been the end of the agency. Not only would I have gone to jail if I had gone along with what the White House wanted us to do, but the agency's credibility would have been ruined forever." In typical Nixonian fashion, efforts to remove Helms from the CIA started immediately, and eventually he lost his job as Director of Central Intelligence in February 1973. As McCord predicted, every tree in the forest would fall with him.

---

[9] U.S. History.com - Watergate Scandal

Helms

Nixon also had to worry about the 1972 presidential election against George McGovern that November. On August 29, Nixon announced that his White House Counsel, John Dean, had investigated the break-in and claimed, "I can say categorically that... no one in the White House staff, no one in this Administration, presently employed, was involved in this very bizarre incident." Nixon further praised Dean on September 15, "The way you've handled it, it seems to me, has been very skillful, because you—putting your fingers in the dikes every time that leaks have sprung here and sprung there." In fact, far from conducting any semblance of an investigation, Dean was actively working to obstruct one by destroying evidence.

Ultimately, the initial coverup efforts were successful through the election. Although more information kept coming out tying the Watergate burglary attempt to men affiliated with CREEP, and financial records also showed the way in which money was being moved, Nixon's reelection campaign was never in jeopardy. Even as indictments were handed down to the five conspirators, Nixon won in a landslide over McGovern, and despite the fact Liddy and McCord were about to be convicted for a wide range of crimes, including burglary and illegal wire-tapping, the coverup successfully contained the full breadth of the White House's work behind the scenes. Of course, if anything, Nixon's historic landslide showed just how needless his Administration's attempts to go after its political enemies were.

Nixon had been reelected, but his problems with Watergate were just beginning.

Chapter 4: Unraveling the Coverup

The Nixon Administration's immediate attempts to coverup the extent of its involvement would not begin to unravel for well over another year. Even though Woodward and Carl Bernstein reported on the scandal throughout the summer and continued to receive information from Deep Throat, connections to the president gained little traction. The *Washington Post* was still isolated in the battle with the White House, and no other major newspapers seemed interested, but despite the advantage of having a direct line to Felt, the two famous reporters have claimed in retrospect that what was received from Deep Throat served mostly to confirm information from other sources. Although Nixon would later claim "Watergate would have been a blip" if he was a Democrat, media interest in the story was initially low; even though Felt also leaked details to other publications like *Time*, most outlets wouldn't really start running with Watergate until they caught wind that one of the men implicated had alleged they were part of a high-profile conspiracy and coverup.

Woodward
(Washington Post)

Gradually, as suspicion grew that the Watergate break-in was a more far-reaching conspiracy, the Senate voted to conduct an investigation following Acting FBI Director Gray's testimony before they confirmed him for the permanent position of FBI Director. His testimony implicated several of the White House staff, and on March 21, 1973, John Dean wrote to the president describing the escalating controversy as "a cancer growing on the presidency." Meanwhile, as the five men arrested for the break-in found themselves being positioned to take the fall, not to mention lengthy prison sentences, they started to make waves as well. Hunt began to make rumblings of confessions that could only be forestalled by hush money, after which he almost immediately received $75,000. Hunt's wife Dorothy was deeply involved as well; on the morning of December 8, 1972, she and her daughter Teresa were killed in a plane crash while carrying $10,000 in $100 bills, all meant to be used as hush money. Hunt and others insisted that it was money for a real estate investment, but before boarding the plane, she purchased a life insurance policy that paid $250,000 upon her death and made her husband beneficiary. Her strange death is a never-ending source of fascination for conspiracy theorists who suspect that she was murdered by the Administration; one such report claims that "moments after impact, a battalion of plainclothes operatives in unmarked cars parked on side streets pounced on the crash site." McCord would later claim in his book, *A Piece of Tape - the Watergate Story: Fact and Fiction*, that Dorothy Hunt possessed information about the president of such magnitude that it would almost certainly result in his impeachment. It is also surprising that in this book, which McCord wasted no time in writing (having it published in 1974), "Former CIA officer Miles Copland claimed that had he [McCord] had led the Watergate burglars into a trap, and that Helms had prior knowledge of the break-in."

The trial began on January 8, 1973 and sported a colorful cast of characters, beginning with Judge John Sirica, a former boxer who was well-known for doling out strict sentences. He had worked in the U.S. Attorney's office during the Hoover administration despite losing his first 13 cases as a court-appointed attorney, and known as a maverick Republican, many of his decisions were later overturned. Considered unpredictable by the legal world, the term "Maximum John" followed him through his career. During the trial, Sirica created an enduring conflict when he met secretly with the Watergate Committee prosecutor, Leon Jaworski, and the judge stirred the pot even more when he took to questioning witnesses himself after finding their testimony uninformative and of dubious integrity.

Meanwhile, in an effort to get ahead of the scandal, the president made a March 1 announcement that he was initiating his own investigation of Watergate, but the day after, he instructed U.S. Attorney General John Mitchell, "I want you to stonewall it; let them plead the Fifth Amendment; cover-up or anything else, if it'll save it; save the plan." By this time, federal agents had already discovered the Nixon administration slush fund to sponsor attacks on various foes of the White House, and the money trail was traced to the top line in the Attorney General's Office: John Mitchell himself. Mitchell was an old law partner of Nixon, and he had also been the commander of John F. Kennedy's PT Boat unit. Before the Watergate affair, he had worked with issues of segregation and affirmative action, but Mitchell would be indicted in May 1973 and convicted of conspiracy to obstruct justice, perjury, and obstruction of justice, ultimately serving 19 months in prison. Before his conviction, Mitchell had tried to get the *Washington Post* to spike a story about the slush fund, warning that Katharine Graham, the *Washington Post*'s publisher, would have a sensitive area of her body "caught in a big fat wringer if that's published."

Mitchell about to testify before the Senate Watergate Committee in 1963

About a month after the beginning of the Watergate trial, on February 7, the Senate voted 77 - 0 to create a Select Committee on Presidential Campaign Activities. The Committee was to be headed by Sam Ervin of North Carolina, who would become a national TV icon thanks to the daily broadcasts from the capital. Although the public perceived of him as a relaxed grandfatherly type, Ervin was a hard-nosed, decorated soldier from World War I and a Harvard Law graduate. Of particular offense to Ervin was Nixon's continued refusal to testify before the committee or to allow his staff to testify, citing executive privilege, national security and any other legal mechanism he could think up. Referring to the Nixon subordinates' refusal to offer information, Ervin was particularly incensed: "Divine right of kings went out with the American Revolution and doesn't belong to White House aides - that is not executive privilege, that is executive poppycock!"

Ervin

It may have been that the hierarchical Nixon felt that he could more successfully exert pressure upon the Watergate prosecutors than on the chairman of the committee, as Ervin seemed impervious to political, social or media press. He was thought by many in the Senate to be the perfect candidate for the job, having gathered enormous respect from both sides of the aisle over his many years of service. His description of the Committee's mandate early on left no doubt as to his intent: "My colleagues on the Committee are determined to uncover all the relevant facts surrounding these matters, and to spare no one, whatever his position in life may be." In subsequent writings about Watergate, which include *The Whole Truth: The Watergate Conspiracy*, *Humor of a Country Lawyer*, and *Preserving the Constitution*, Ervin expressed one major regret regarding the outcome of the proceedings: "Congress did not do more to restrict the president's executive privilege."

The president would seemingly have had a better chance with the Assistant Chairman of the Watergate Committee, Republican Howard Baker of Tennessee, but Baker was able to conduct himself properly throughout, awkward as it might have been for him. Nixon's campaign literature for 1972 hailed Baker as a trusted friend and advisor to the president, but Baker never hindered Ervin's relentless pursuit of the president and his staff. In fact, it was Baker who coined the famous phrase, "What did the President know, and when did he know it?"

As the investigations were beginning, Nixon started to see that more proactive steps were necessary, but another big blow came in the middle of March. The Watergate incident might have died out without reaching the executive level had not John McCord written his personal note to Judge Sirica on March 19, based on the probability that he faced an extensive prison term after initially refusing to cooperate. After the attempt to strong-arm the CIA, which had resulted in the sacking of Richard Helms, McCord was entirely isolated with no protection, so he followed through with his previous threat against the president to abandon the collective secrecy of the action and tell all.

His letter to Judge Sirica was filed in *United States v. George Gordon Libby* in the District Court of Washington, D.C., and opened simply, "to Judge Sirica." In the sudden change to a cooperative tone, McCord cited the conflicting circumstances in which he was trapped, describing himself as "whipsawed in a variety of legalities." Among these, he included the possibility of future testimony being required of him before the Senate Committee, becoming the object of a later civil suit, and of his testimony becoming a matter of record within the Senate via the probation officer, specifically confidential communications between judge and defendant. McCord qualified these sentiments, however, by citing that "on the other hand, to fail to answer your questions may appear to be non-cooperation, and I can therefore expect a much more severe sentence."[10] McCord added alleged fears on the part of his family for his safety and well-being, and although he claimed not to share it, he did express an expectation of certain retaliations against those close to him: "Such retaliations could destroy careers, income, and reputations of persons who are innocent of any guilt whatever."[11]

McCord continued by itemizing certain truths which he felt were not possible to divulge in public testimony due to pressure exerted upon the defendants by those at the federal level. The first item was quoted directly: "There was political pressure applied to defendants to plead guilty and remain silent." The second point was a claim that perjury had been committed by the defendants "in matters highly material to the very structure, orientation and impact of the government's case, and to the motivation and intent of the defendants."[12]

---

[10] Watergate.info - James McCord
[11] Watergate. info - James McCord

McCord's third point was that certain individuals were not identified in courtroom testimony that could have been identified by those testifying. He further claimed that although the Cuban participants might have been led to believe that Watergate was a CIA operation, he knew for a fact that it was not. In another point, McCord described one individual's testimony as a case of "honest errors of memory," although the testifier was perceived as telling untruths. Finally, he explained his previous actions as subject to the circumstances under which his defense was forced to be prepared.

His agenda fully itemized, McCord requested a private meeting in chambers with Sirica following the sentencing phase, and that his speaking with an FBI agent or before a grand jury (and the attending U.S. Attorneys) or other government representatives would be unacceptable. He maintained that no discussion involving such a meeting had taken place with his attorneys, for the sake of their protection, and that he offered his statement "freely and voluntarily."[13] In his time before the committee, McCord offered testimony on many of the accomplished and planned actions underwritten by the White House.

Thus, in his letter to Sirica, McCord had claimed that the defendants were pressured by White House staff to plead guilty and avoid being forthcoming on any salient point of the event. He further charged that the defendants had been forced to perjure themselves for "higher-ups." This letter changed the course of Watergate in two ways. First, the event brought the break-in outside of the Washington beltway and fueled the larger public imagination, and second, it changed the face of Watergate from a criminal investigation to a political bombshell. The *Washington Post* would never again find itself alone in its interest.

In mid-April, Jeb Magruder was feeling the heat, and in turn he implicated John Dean and Attorney General John Mitchell. In turn, just a few days later, John Dean informed Nixon that he too was now cooperating with authorities, and that same day, authorities informed the Administration that Haldeman, Ehrlichman, Dean and others had all been implicated as part of a high-level coverup. Naturally, in an effort to distance himself from them, Nixon asked these White House officials to resign. By separating from them, he hoped he could turn any subsequent investigations into his own actions as being his word against theirs.

One of the items that unnerved John Dean the most was McCord's letter to Judge Sirica, and he began to warn Nixon repeatedly that things were getting out of control, as "his resolve wilted." Shortly after, Dean agreed to cooperate with prosecutors on April 6 under an agreement of limited immunity. Within his testimony of the following month would be a claim that he had discussed the workings of a cover-up with the President himself. In fact, he estimated that he had discussed it with Nixon approximately 35 times.

---

[12] Watergate.info
[13] Watergate.info

The straightforwardness of Dean's testimony could be ascribed to a number of motivations, from a sense of conscience to the strategy of being coolly truthful and not overplaying the nobility of breaking open the corruption. When Senator Talmedge commented to Dean in session that "in finding evidence of a conspirator of this magnitude, it was incumbent upon you as a counsel to the president that he got that information at the time," Dean simply responded, "Senator, I was participating in a cover-up at that time."[14] When asked in the same session whether Dean felt that his conscience was clear, his answer combined ethics and self-survival, claiming that he "could not endure perjury upon perjury upon perjury...I wasn't capable of doing that, and I knew that my day of being called was not far off."[15]

In addition to his conversations with the president, Dean suggested a similar body of conversations with Patrick Gray, Assistant Director of the FBI, on the same subject. Gray had admitted such in the hearings for his appointment to Director of the FBI, and his nomination was ultimately rejected. Dean's first day testimony of seven hours not only clearly implicated the president in the cover-up but was the first bald assertion that the subject of the cover-up could be found in presidential conversations on the White House tapes.

A few months into 1973, Nixon was confident that he was almost done with Watergate and would soon never have to speak of it again, but he now realized he had to take more proactive steps. On April 17, the president announced that in a change of heart, his staff would appear before the Watergate Committee, although the same reticence to testify would hold true. The same day, Nixon claimed that he had no prior knowledge of the incident on any level. And on April 30, Nixon announced the resignations of Dean, Haldeman, and Ehrlichman, stating, "In one of the most difficult decisions of my Presidency, I accepted the resignations of two of my closest associates in the White House, Bob Haldeman, John Ehrlichman, two of the finest public servants it has been my privilege to know. Because Attorney General Kleindienst, though a distinguished public servant, my personal friend for 20 years, with no personal involvement whatsoever in this matter has been a close personal and professional associate of some of those who are involved in this case, he and I both felt that it was also necessary to name a new Attorney General. The Counsel to the President, John Dean, has also resigned." After the speech, Nixon was quoted as consoling Haldeman, "Well, it's a tough thing, Bob, for you, for John, and the rest...but goddamnit, I'm never going to discuss this son-of-a-bitch Watergate thing again...never, never, never, never."

Chapter 5: Catching Up With Nixon

As the links widened and pointed toward consistent executive involvement, containment

---

[14] NBClearn
[15] NBClearn[15]
[15] NBClearn

became exponentially more difficult, and it seemed as though every new instance of the White House digging in its heels was met with a new revelation causing circumstances to slip out of its control. On June 13, a memo was discovered in which Ehrlichman's plans to break-into the office of Daniel Ellsberg's psychiatrist was discovered, and John Dean's seven-hour statement to the committee had already turned Nixon into the committee's principal target, not to mention his own testimony. As late as July 7, Nixon still refused to appear before the panel, and rejected all demands for presidential documents.

This latest stalemate, however, was broken wide open by the discovery of the president's secret taping system in the White House, one previously employed by John F. Kennedy. The taping system had been implemented to archive the thoughts of all those in White House meetings, but now it was clearly a key piece of evidence that would clearly show the president's depth of involvement. The knowledge of a taping system was somewhat innocently explained to the committee by former White House Appointments Secretary Alexander Butterfield, and it was quickly discovered that the tapes of White House meetings and calls went back to 1971.

By now, the sentiment that the Watergate break-in was not nearly as serious as the White House coverup became a rallying cry for large anti-White House segments of the population, and for the committee. Those intent on tracing the crime to the top of the executive branch smelled blood. On August 15, Nixon was before the cameras again, this time extolling before the public the importance of confidentiality in executive dealings, but over the next several weeks, the two years of taped presidential conversations occupied the center of the investigations. Even as they became the object of a subpoena, Nixon disconnected the system on July 26, a week before the subpoena for the tapes.

Not surprisingly, Nixon's August appearance made little difference to the judiciary, and Judge Sirica demanded that the White House turn over the entire collection on August 29. The committee continued to insist that he turn them over as well, having won every legal step toward taking possession of them thus far.

As the legal arguments over that subpoena were ongoing, Nixon lost his strongest attack dog on October 10 with the resignation of Vice President Spiro Agnew, who resigned his office after pleading no contest to charges of income tax evasion. A Marylander, Agnew was a popular choice for the ticket in the South. At first glance, his inclusion as an attack dog against various opposition groups fit Nixon's combative style perfectly, but he also bypassed the opportunity for gaining favor and winning friends, something at which Nixon was extraordinarily clumsy. Before allegations of fraudulent financial practices hit Agnew, he symbolized the righteousness of the administration, lashing out at the anti-war movement, but unfortunately, he did not stop at what was considered a nation-wide adolescent rebellion. So pervasive were his tirades, written for the most part by speechwriters Pat Buchanan and William Safire, that he took on the persona of "a tough-talking, intensely negative public presence in Washington." [16] His descriptions of collegiate protesters as "an effete corps of impudent snobs who characterize themselves as intellectuals...[who] take their tactics from Fidel Castro and their money from daddy" resonated with middle-aged and older Americans. Attacking the national press, however, was damaging to a faction much needed by the Administration.

Still, Agnew's alliterative descriptions of the "nattering nabobs of negativism" caught the public fascination, even though he was disliked. One Baltimore patron, asked whether he hoped Agnew would become president, responded that he didn't want a president who sounded like he did after a few beers. Railing against general enemies of the White House, Agnew employed phrases such as "pusillanimous pussy-footers," "vicars of vacillation" and ideological eunuchs." Even these lines were crossed, however, as the Baltimore street-talking style entered the arena of racial slurs against several groups, including Asians and Poles.

In time, even Nixon himself realized that Agnew, a regular complainer about the disrespect he felt in the White House, was a liability, and so he pressured Agnew to resign. Agnew resisted at first, and he even blamed White House staff for conspiring against him. Nixon attempted to replace him with Texas Governor John Connally, a victim (and hero) of the Kennedy assassination, but Connally wasn't interested in the office, calling it "useless." Agnew eventually agreed to resign if provided with guarantees against being prosecuted.

Thus, with Agnew out, on October 12th, Gerald Ford was nominated to replace Agnew, the very same day the U.S. Circuit Court of Appeals ruled that the entire body of tapes must be turned over. The man who had subpoenaed the tapes was Special Prosecutor Archibald Cox, who had been the eighth person sought out by Attorney General Elliott Richardson for the position of Special Prosecutor. Cox was Richardson's old law professor, and Cox's great-grandfather, William Maxwell Evarts, had defended Andrew Johnson in his impeachment, barely saving him from conviction. In Cox, Nixon would find yet another obstacle that he could not move via political or legal bullying, and he also harbored a particular mistrust of Cox due to his ties to the Kennedys, as the Prosecutor had served as an advisor for Congressman John F. Kennedy over a decade earlier. Cox had no intention of budging on the White House's compromise of edited tapes, particularly since the editing was to be done by one of Nixon's people, and on top of that, the president further stipulated that Cox would call for no further evidence.

[16] History Common

Cox

Nixon viewed Cox as an increasing menace and attempted to remove him, thinking that the head of the committee being absent might lessen the pressure. This led to a series of severe White House actions in the month of October, culminating in what came to be known as the Saturday Night Massacre. Nixon desperately sought some high-ranking official in the judicial system who would forcibly remove Archibald Cox from the Senate Committee. The president personally called Attorney General Elliott Richardson and instructed him to make the firing happen. When the Attorney General refused, he was fired over the phone. Following that, the president called the Assistant Attorney General, William Ruckelshaus, who also refused and was fired. At last, someone was found who would do the deed: Acting Attorney General Robert Bork. Bork removed Cox from the committee. Clearly, Bork had learned from the previous two men being fired that his ability to stay in office required following the president's order, though he later claimed he considered resigning to avoid being "perceived as a man who did the President's bidding to save my job." Regardless, he appointed Leon Jaworski to take Cox's place.

The "Massacre" received widespread public criticism, and the first serious calls for the president's impeachment were now beginning heard. The following week, an irate Congress called for impeachment as well, introducing 22 resolutions to that effect. Cox was elevated to the level of an American hero, "the last honest man in Washington". Again, the president had exercised his skill in retaliation, but he had utterly neglected to garner support, either inside or outside of the Beltway. Cox's official response to his removal was terse; invoking John Adams, he said, "Whether ours shall continue to be a government of laws and not men is now before

Congress and ultimately before the American people."[17]

On October 23, with the walls closing in on him, Nixon appeared to relent by releasing a portion of the tapes, but it was quickly apparent that none of these tapes had any significant pertinence to the matter at hand. At this point, a series of suspicious irregularities occurred, such as claims that specific tapes on the list did not exist. The famous 18 minute gap, when investigated, met with conflicting answers from secretary Rosemary Woods and other White House officials. Chief of Staff Alexander Haig "credited the gap to 'some sinister force,'"[18] which he did not specify. Regardless, the announcement of an 18 minute gap, suggesting five separate erasures, was announced by the White House on November 21. Woods, the curator of the tapes, denied any involvement in the missing archives.

Ultimately, firing Cox led Nixon nowhere. When Jaworski took over for Archibald Cox on November 1, via an appointment made by Robert Bork (former Solicitor General and third in line behind the Attorney General), he proved to be every bit as insistent as his predecessor, and he immediately called for full disclosure of the tapes.

Jaworski

In the month of November, the tug-of-war continued between the judicial and executive branches, and following the Christmas break, the House of Representatives instructed the Judiciary Committee to investigate the viability of impeachment against the president, congruent

---

[17] The Washington Post; *Archibald Cox* - www.washingtonpost.com
[18] Gerald R. Ford Library and Museum

with all the other investigations then taking place with the court case, Jaworski and the committee. By the beginning of March, seven White House aides had been indicted on 13 counts of obstructing an investigation. Nixon being named by Jaworski as an "un-indicted co-conspirator" did not place the president in immediate jeopardy, but it was lethal in terms of public opinion.

The president released the previously offered transcripts, heavily edited, and followed their emergence with another television appearance, much like the last one. However, with the materials that had come out, however, Nixon's likeability among the larger population was taking an enormous hit, due in no small part to the unexpected vulgarity of his language on the recordings. From this collective realization came the now famous phrase "expletive deleted." An editorial in the *Chicago Tribune* complained, "He is humorless to the point of being inhumane. He is devious. He is vacillating. He is profane. He is willing to be led. He displays dismaying gaps in knowledge. He is suspicious of his staff. His loyalty is minimal."

Nixon knew, without a doubt, that the process of impeachment, initiated by the House and tried by the Senate, not only depended on high crimes and misdemeanors but the detailed documentation of such. The physical possession of the tapes was essential to that distinction, for without such a level of evidence, "the linkage between presidential misdemeanors performed by the president is neither automatic nor obvious."[19] Even at this late date, he believed he was able to control them. What he was no longer able to manipulate, however, despite a history of brilliant game-saving television appearances, was public opinion and various factions of institutional support. He certainly was aware that "other things being equal, popular presidents are more capable of enduring accusations," With the tapes given up and with the new public perception of his personal style, Nixon had spent or wasted his remaining political capital.

Impeachment hearings began in early March of 1974 in the Judiciary, assisted by material provided by Sirica's court. Jaworski, meanwhile, "appealed to the Supreme Court to force Nixon to surrender more tapes."[20] A decision was not received until July 24, but by a vote of 8 - 0, the court upheld the request for the turnover of the tapes. Quickly after that, three articles of impeachment came down from the House: "Obstructing the Watergate investigation; misuse of power and violating the oath of office; failure to comply with House subpoenas."[21]

Finally, on the 5th of August, Nixon released the remaining tapes, but only after considering far more rash last-minute actions against the Supreme Court. All in all, the White House tapes cover a period of "2 years - 3700 hours of phone calls and meetings. 2,371 are declassified."[22] Highlighted conversations, now available on many internet sources, include brashly profane and

---

[19] Victor J. Hinohosa, Anibal S. Perez-Linan, "Presidential Survival and the Impeachment Process", in *Political Science Quarterly* Vol. 121, no. 4 Winter 2006, p.655

[20] Gerald R. Ford Library and Museum

[21] Gerald R. Ford Library and Museum

[22] Nixontapes.org

vulgar attempts on the president's part to both understand what is happening to him and to control it through the force of his office. The most important tapes, now available for listen all over the internet, include the "smoking gun" conversation of June 23, 1972, a conversation about tracing money back to the White House from those bills found in the burglars' possession. Other important recordings include the January 1973 excerpt in which Charles Colson explains why George McGovern had to be bugged, the March 21 "Cancer on the presidency" warnings of John Dean, including discussion of hush money payments to Hunt and others. In that one, Nixon suggests the blackmail money should be paid: "…just looking at the immediate problem, don't you have to have – handle Hunt's financial situation damn soon? […] you've got to keep the cap on the bottle that much, in order to have any options." There is also the March 27 discussion of John Mitchell's involvement, and an April 16 discussion on how to stall the investigation and deal with the Dean problem. More tapes continue to be declassified, including as recently as 340 hours in 2013.

Of the released tapes, one of the first to receive recognition was recorded only a few days after the break-in: the "smoking gun" conversation with H.R. Haldeman that was damning enough for Nixon's remaining support in the Senate to crumble. In it, Haldeman can be heard telling Nixon, "the Democratic break-in thing, we're back to the–in the, the problem area because the FBI is not under control, because Gray doesn't exactly know how to control them, and they have… their investigation is now leading into some productive areas […] and it goes in some directions we don't want it to go." With that, as Fred Buzhardt and James St. Clair put it, "The tape proved that the President had lied to the nation, to his closest aides, and to his own lawyers – for more than two years."

On the night of August 7, several Congressmen, including Senators Barry Goldwater and Hugh Scott, met with Nixon to tell him that he would certainly be impeached in the House and convicted in the Senate. Thus, the next day, the president announced his resignation from office:

> "In all the decisions I have made in my public life, I have always tried to do what was best for the Nation. Throughout the long and difficult period of Watergate, I have felt it was my duty to persevere, to make every possible effort to complete the term of office to which you elected me. In the past few days, however, it has become evident to me that I no longer have a strong enough political base in the Congress to justify continuing that effort. As long as there was such a base, I felt strongly that it was necessary to see the constitutional process through to its conclusion, that to do otherwise would be unfaithful to the spirit of that deliberately difficult process and a dangerously destabilizing precedent for the future....
>
> I would have preferred to carry through to the finish whatever the personal agony it would have involved, and my family unanimously urged me to do so. But the interest of the Nation must always come before any personal considerations. From

the discussions I have had with Congressional and other leaders, I have concluded that because of the Watergate matter I might not have the support of the Congress that I would consider necessary to back the very difficult decisions and carry out the duties of this office in the way the interests of the Nation would require.

I have never been a quitter. To leave office before my term is completed is abhorrent to every instinct in my body. But as President, I must put the interest of America first. America needs a full-time President and a full-time Congress, particularly at this time with problems we face at home and abroad. To continue to fight through the months ahead for my personal vindication would almost totally absorb the time and attention of both the President and the Congress in a period when our entire focus should be on the great issues of peace abroad and prosperity without inflation at home. Therefore, I shall resign the Presidency effective at noon tomorrow. Vice President Ford will be sworn in as President at that hour in this office."

As a result of Watergate, 69 government officials would be indicted, and 48 would be convicted of some crime. Among all the White House conspirators, Richard Nixon remained free of further court actions, thanks to a full pardon the following year from then President Gerald R. Ford. Ford justified that controversial decision by calling Nixon's plight and potential ongoing criminal investigation "an American tragedy in which we all have played a part. It could go on and on and on, or someone must write the end to it. I have concluded that only I can do that, and if I can, I must."

A 1976 campaign button referencing Ford's pardon of Nixon

Chapter 6: The Impact of Watergate

Calmer voices, such as that of the steady-minded Adlai Stevenson, refer to the Watergate era as one "in which we reacted not to history, but to aberrations of history." The decade is viewed as one in which great institutional shifts took place, and one in which executive powers were wrested from the presidency in general. In retrospect, much is said of the networking of the White House staff; where they were once designed to sustain efficiency, the 1970s increasingly turned them into an institutional mover of policy, political gamesmanship, camouflage and deflection. George Reedy, two years before the Watergate break-in, warned that "one of Mr. Nixon's biggest mistakes was in enlarging the White House Staff."[23]

Author Walter Lippman suggested that corruption in national governments represents a fairly steady topography, but that " a community governs itself by fits and starts of unsuspecting complacency and violent suspicion." All this is to say that the Nixon administration thrived during a period of the latter, and Victor Lasky agreed with that view in "It Didn't Start with Watergate" (1977), suggesting that Richard Nixon was in no way unusual and that all the events occurring in that era had occurred regularly before. Pro-Nixon conservatives, who observed the rise in reporter freedom among the nation's major newspapers and the media's ability to diminish the integrity of public figures through rabid journalism by rooting out "public

---

[23] Gordon Hoxie, *Presidential Studies Quarterly*

misconduct," claim that the habit had its origins during the Taft and Theodore Roosevelt administrations, impelled by "professional writers who portrayed themselves as objective servers of society, reporting conditions as they found them."

Former Nixon official Geoff Shepard, in his book *The Secret Plot to Make Ted Kennedy President*, claimed that Watergate as a whole was much more about Democratic political maneuvering than it was about White House crimes, and that Sirica's improprieties were blatant, as he met with the Watergate Special Prosecutor in a behind-the-scenes farce of "secret meetings, secret documents, [and] secret collusion."[24] He suggests overall that no fair trials were ever received or intended, and that the real intent of the proceedings was to gain a stronger hold on Congress and injure the Republican party beyond repair. The book, in fact, is dedicated "to the thousands of Republicans...whose aspirations were thwarted, whose careers were ended, and whose lives were ruined in the single-minded effort to destroy them and the GOP - to the end that Ted Kennedy might become president, and the restoration of Camelot finally be achieved."[25]

Whichever side of the press debate one is on, it is undeniable that national press, in particular the *Washington Post*, brought the otherwise small incident of an office burglary to light, and it is commonly thought that if the *Post* had not served as David to the White House's Goliath, the whole thing might very well have blown over. The question of why the incident did not die a quick and mostly overlooked death endures; by September 1972, only 52% of the public had even heard of the Watergate break-in, but by June of 1973, almost all Americans were intimately aware of both the incident and of the ongoing judicial process. George McGovern made corruption a theme in his presidential campaign in 1972, but even then, he did not specifically address Watergate, and by 1974, the energy crisis in America could very easily have served as the replacement story to an already aging Watergate saga.

In some quarters, among liberals and journalists, the press is hailed as an enormous moving force, and in most cases, a heroic one. Conversely, others believe to this day that the press did not play more than a modest role in ending the Nixon administration. Regardless, there was an additional reason for the *Washington Post* holding the inside track on the Watergate investigation. Not only did they function centrally within the Beltway, but they had an unimaginably fortuitous source within the top levels of government, one of which no other journalistic institution could boast. Martin Kalb, of Harvard's Shorenstein Center of the Press, Politics and Public Policy, believed that the *Washington Post*'s general push to air deeper aspects of the scandal was "absolutely critical to creating an atmosphere in Washington and within the government that Nixon was in serious trouble, and that the White House was engaged in a cover-up."[26] Indeed, it was the refusal to back down or let go of the subject that Woodward and Bernstein, representing the Post in the face of numerous federal threats, kept the pursuit of the

---

[24] Geoff Shepard, "The Secret Plot to Make Ted Kennedy President: Inside the *Real* Watergate Conspiracy, Penguin Group: New York, 2008
[25] Geoff Shepard, "The Secret Plot to Make Ted Kennedy President: The *Real* Watergate Conspiracy"
[26] Mark Feldstein, *Watergate Revisited,* aijarchive.com, 2004-www.aijarchive.org/article.asp?id=3735

scandal's hidden layers moving forward. According to one pro-journalist source, Woodward and Bernstein "produced the single most spectacular act of serious journalism [in the 20th century]."[27] And of course, Woodward and Bernstein eventually published the defining book of the era on the subject, *All the President's Men*, which was sensationalized in a film with Robert Redmond and Dustin Hoffman and captured the public's fascination with "Deep Throat," a clearly well-informed source whose identity would remain secret for nearly 30 years after the events in question.

As the Watergate era fades into history, it is surprising how many of the important players who remain are still active as journalists, biographers and activists. Of course, the central figure in the scandal, Richard Nixon, suffered a stroke in 1994 and died shortly after, but one of his most important victims, Daniel Ellsberg, the leaker of the Pentagon Papers, occupies a nobler place in modern society than he once did (though his status as a traitor or hero for "delegitimizing" the Vietnam War have vehement advocates on both sides of the question). Like many involved in the Watergate era, he continued to work as an activist and was at one point arrested in an Iraq War protest. He consistently lends support to modern "leakers" of government documents, including Edward Snowden, and almost without exception is pro-transparency.

The important White House source who contributed so much primary knowledge to the work of Woodward and Bernstein, Mark Felt, died in 2008 at the age of 95. Felt witnessed the beginnings of modern technology and all the recent events and discoveries of the modern age. Convicted for pursuing alleged members of the Weather Underground without warrants on repeated occasions, he was pardoned by then President Ronald Reagan. Woodward and Bernstein had agreed to keep his identity anonymous, but that became unnecessary when Felt announced himself as Deep Throat in 2005 and continued to release information at the urging of his family.

In terms of mystery and fascination over the scandal, E. Howard Hunt may be the most enigmatic character of the entire era, even more than Deep Throat. Known as the "ultimate keeper of secrets," Hunt died in Miami, January 23, 2007, of pneumonia. Hedegaard alleges that Hunt spent ten years as a meth dealer, and twenty as an addict, living in a state of bitterness that, in his view, the country had punished him for what they trained and instructed him to do. The elusive "final confessions" to his children were at some point intended to answer the question of who killed John F. Kennedy, and one of his sons has reason to believe, entirely unfounded by hard and public evidence, that the deed was perpetrated by his father.

Hunt's overseer at the White House, H.R. Haldeman, died of abdominal cancer in Santa Barbara, in 1993. He served a total of 18 months for his part in the Watergate affair, after which he reestablished himself as a highly successful businessman, dealing mostly in high end real estate. His colleague, John Ehrlichman, outlived him by six years, dying in Atlanta in 1999. He

---

[27] Mark Feldstein, *Watergate Revisited*,

served one and-a-half years for the scandal, after which he worked as an artist and as a prodigious novelist.

G. Gordon Libby, who had worked as an agent for the FBI and the Treasury, served as legal counsel to CREEP, and was codenamed "Gemstone," ultimately served under five months of prison time and was given a large fine. Liddy continued as a popular radio host through 2012, after writing the autobiographical *Will*, in which he claims to have planned the murder of columnist Jack Anderson. At the age of 84, he has not been widely seen or heard in public since 2012.

Of all the Watergate conspirators, there is only one who never broke ranks with the president and never wrote memoirs or anything revealing his personal knowledge of the scandal. John Mitchell was the ultimate Nixon loyalist until his death from a heart attack in 1988. He served 19 months in prison until he was paroled due to a medical condition. On the day of his parole, "he told reporters who gathered to greet him, 'From henceforth, don't call me. I'll call you.' He never called."[28]

The judge in the Watergate trials, John Sirica, died on August 15, 1992 of cardiac arrest. During his professional years, he did not comment extensively on the trial, but in his book, *To Set the Record Straight*, he made it clear that "Nixon should have been indicted after leaving the presidency for his part in the Watergate cover-up."[29]

James McCord, one of the five who directly participated in the burglary of the Democratic National Committee in the Watergate hotel, has remained anonymous to a greater degree of success than many of his colleagues. Entering his 90th year, the White House electronics expert has not been heard from after several of his works as an author were published.

The "evil genius" of the Nixon administration, Charles "Chuck" Colson, died of a brain hemorrhage in 2012. Following the Watergate era, he became an evangelical minister, which included an extensive prison ministry. In 2000, Jeb Bush restored his right to vote.

John Dean, White house Counsel to President Nixon, is an activist and author, taking aim in particular at conservative Republican agendas and key individuals. He promoted the impeachment of George W. Bush for the Iraq War, but following his role in Watergate, he was disbarred and has never practiced law again. When asked why he made no effort to regain his license to practice, he stated that he never wanted to pursue that line of work again, that it was a "been there, done that."

Leon Jaworski, the second Special Prosecutor, was a presidential appointment, but Nixon might have thought better about keeping Archibald Cox after encountering Jaworski's tenacity,

---

[28] Lawrence Meyer Washington Post, "John Mitchell, Watergate, Dies at 75"

[29] Bart Barnes, Washington Post, "John Sirica, Watergate Judge, Dies", August 15, 1992

gathered in various legal settings around the United States and as a war-time prosecutor in Germany. Jaworski died in 1982 at his ranch in Wimberley, Texas, while chopping wood.

The famous attack-dog Vice President, Spiro Agnew, rebounded from the Watergate experience in short order, reinventing himself in international trader with numerous mansions in far-flung locations. He died in 1998 at the age of 77 from a sudden onset of previously undiscovered leukemia and is buried in Timonium, Maryland. Despite his strained relations with the president, he was invited to Nixon's funeral and attended. The Nixon daughters returned the favor at his death.

Bob Woodward continues to write privately and contribute to the Washington Post, as does his colleague, Carl Bernstein. In June 2012, Woodward and Bernstein collaborated on a retrospective article in memory of the White House answer four days after the break-in: "'Certain elements may try to stretch this beyond what it is.' press secretary Ronald Ziegler scoffed, dismissing the incident as a 'third-rate burglary.'" The pair go on to describe the entire presidency of Richard Nixon as being embodied within the Watergate mentality, implying that the bulk of his term was spent in vicious retaliation against attacks coming from his most oppositional factions: "In the course of his five-and-a-half year presidency,...Nixon launched and managed five successive, overlapping wars - the anti-Vietnam War movement, the news media, the Democrats, the Justice System and finally, against history itself."

This would certainly represent the liberal view of Nixon's legacy, but unanimity in such matters is impossible, especially as the years go by. In specific polling among the American population, not only have Watergate and the administration of Richard Nixon parted ways, despite a universal knowledge that they are inextricably linked at the literal level, but Nixon himself has been compartmentalized as being among the greatest foreign policy presidents in history, and among the most troubling from a standpoint of corruption. in 1976, 63% deemed him to be the most immoral postwar president, yet in 1986, 12% responded that Nixon was one of the greatest presidents, and he is almost always ranked in the top two for international affairs., where the vastly more popular Kennedy is not.

Richard Nixon had only reached the presidency after successfully figuring out ways to reinvent himself, overcoming one professional setback after another during his long political career. A man of considerable intellect and fierce personal determination, he amply demonstrated the potential power of the presidency to act unilaterally within the nation's internal affairs. In that sense, he did Americans a favor through the constitutional and social crisis of Watergate by forcing the following generation to question the balance between the three branches of government, to carefully consider which conditions should allow one branch to take command over another, to monitor the boundaries of support staff, and to expand the debate over government transparency and official privilege. That said, no matter how many times people point out that he "opened China", Nixon will always have Watergate as a millstone around his neck, and deservedly so. In 1995, 57% of those polled believed "Nixon's influence on American moral values to be negative."[30]

Nixon's Resignation Speech

"Good evening.

This is the 37th time I have spoken to you from this office, where so many decisions have been made that shaped the history of this Nation. Each time I have done so to discuss with you some matter that I believe affected the national interest.

In all the decisions I have made in my public life, I have always tried to do what was best for the Nation. Throughout the long and difficult period of Watergate, I have felt it was my duty to persevere, to make every possible effort to complete the term of office to which you elected me.

In the past few days, however, it has become evident to me that I no longer have a strong enough political base in the Congress to justify continuing that effort. As long as there was such a base, I felt strongly that it was necessary to see the constitutional process through to its conclusion, that to do otherwise would be unfaithful to the spirit of that deliberately difficult process and a dangerously destabilizing precedent for the future.

But with the disappearance of that base, I now believe that the constitutional purpose has been served, and there is no longer a need for the process to be prolonged.

I would have preferred to carry through to the finish whatever the personal agony it would have involved, and my family unanimously urged me to do so. But the interest of the Nation must always come before any personal considerations.

From the discussions I have had with Congressional and other leaders, I have concluded that because of the Watergate matter I might not have the support of the Congress that I would consider necessary to back the very difficult decisions and carry out the duties of this office in the way the interests of the Nation would require.

I have never been a quitter. To leave office before my term is completed is abhorrent to every instinct in my body. But as President, I must put the interest of America first. America needs a full-time President and a full-time Congress, particularly at this time with problems we face at home and abroad.

To continue to fight through the months ahead for my personal vindication would almost totally absorb the time and attention of both the President and the Congress in a period when our entire focus should be on the great issues of peace abroad and prosperity without inflation at

---

[30] Nixon Postmortem, *Annals of the American Academy of Political and Social Science*. Vol. 560 No. 1988, p. 98

home.

==Therefore, I shall resign the Presidency effective at noon tomorrow. Vice President Ford will be sworn in as President at that hour in this office.==

As I recall the high hopes for America with which we began this second term, I feel a great sadness that I will not be here in this office working on your behalf to achieve those hopes in the next 2 1/2 years. But in turning over direction of the Government to Vice President Ford, I know, as I told the Nation when I nominated him for that office 10 months ago, that the leadership of America will be in good hands.

In passing this office to the Vice President, I also do so with the profound sense of the weight of responsibility that will fall on his shoulders tomorrow and, therefore, of the understanding, the patience, the cooperation he will need from all Americans.

As he assumes that responsibility, he will deserve the help and the support of all of us. As we look to the future, the first essential is to begin healing the wounds of this Nation, to put the bitterness and divisions of the recent past behind us, and to rediscover those shared ideals that lie at the heart of our strength and unity as a great and as a free people.

By taking this action, I hope that I will have hastened the start of that process of healing which is so desperately needed in America.

I regret deeply any injuries that may have been done in the course of the events that led to this decision. I would say only that if some of my Judgments were wrong, and some were wrong, they were made in what I believed at the time to be the best interest of the Nation.

To those who have stood with me during these past difficult months, to my family, my friends, to many others who joined in supporting my cause because they believed it was right, I will be eternally grateful for your support.

And to those who have not felt able to give me your support, let me say I leave with no bitterness toward those who have opposed me, because all of us, in the final analysis, have been concerned with the good of the country, however our judgments might differ.

So, let us all now join together in affirming that common commitment and in helping our new President succeed for the benefit of all Americans.

I shall leave this office with regret at not completing my term, but with gratitude for the privilege of serving as your President for the past 5 1/2 years. These years have been a momentous time in the history of our Nation and the world. They have been a time of achievement in which we can all be proud, achievements that represent the shared efforts of the Administration, the Congress, and the people.

But the challenges ahead are equally great, and they, too, will require the support and the efforts of the Congress and the people working in cooperation with the new Administration.

We have ended America's longest war, but in the work of securing a lasting peace in the world, the goals ahead are even more far-reaching and more difficult. We must complete a structure of peace so that it will be said of this generation, our generation of Americans, by the people of all nations, not only that we ended one war but that we prevented future wars.

We have unlocked the doors that for a quarter of a century stood between the United States and the People's Republic of China.

We must now ensure that the one quarter of the world's people who live in the People's Republic of China will be and remain not our enemies but our friends.

In the Middle East, 100 million people in the Arab countries, many of whom have considered us their enemy for nearly 20 years, now look on us as their friends. We must continue to build on that friendship so that peace can settle at last over the Middle East and so that the cradle of civilization will not become its grave.

Together with the Soviet Union we have made the crucial breakthroughs that have begun the process of limiting nuclear arms. But we must set as our goal not just limiting but reducing and finally destroying these terrible weapons so that they cannot destroy civilization and so that the threat of nuclear war will no longer hang over the world and the people.

We have opened the new relation with the Soviet Union. We must continue to develop and expand that new relationship so that the two strongest nations of the world will live together in cooperation rather than confrontation.

Around the world, in Asia, in Africa, in Latin America, in the Middle East, there are millions of people who live in terrible poverty, even starvation. We must keep as our goal turning away from production for war and expanding production for peace so that people everywhere on this earth can at last look forward in their children's time, if not in our own time, to having the necessities for a decent life.

Here in America, we are fortunate that most of our people have not only the blessings of liberty but also the means to live full and good and, by the world's standards, even abundant lives. We must press on, however, toward a goal of not only more and better jobs but of full opportunity for every American and of what we are striving so hard right now to achieve, prosperity without inflation.

For more than a quarter of a century in public life I have shared in the turbulent history of this era. I have fought for what I believed in. I have tried to the best of my ability to discharge those duties and meet those responsibilities that were entrusted to me.

Sometimes I have succeeded and sometimes I have failed, but always I have taken heart from what Theodore Roosevelt once said about the man in the arena, "whose face is marred by dust and sweat and blood, who strives valiantly, who errs and comes short again and again because there is not effort without error and shortcoming, but who does actually strive to do the deed, who knows the great enthusiasms, the great devotions, who spends himself in a worthy cause, who at the best knows in the end the triumphs of high achievements and who at the worst, if he fails, at least fails while daring greatly."

I pledge to you tonight that as long as I have a breath of life in my body, I shall continue in that spirit. I shall continue to work for the great causes to which I have been dedicated throughout my years as a Congressman, a Senator, a Vice President, and President, the cause of peace not just for America but among all nations, prosperity, justice, and opportunity for all of our people.

There is one cause above all to which I have been devoted and to which I shall always be devoted for as long as I live.

When I first took the oath of office as President 5 1/2 years ago, I made this sacred commitment, to "consecrate my office, my energies, and all the wisdom I can summon to the cause of peace among nations."

I have done my very best in all the days since to be true to that pledge. As a result of these efforts, I am confident that the world is a safer place today, not only for the people of America but for the people of all nations, and that all of our children have a better chance than before of living in peace rather than dying in war.

This, more than anything, is what I hoped to achieve when I sought the Presidency. This, more than anything, is what I hope will be my legacy to you, to our country, as I leave the Presidency.

To have served in this office is to have felt a very personal sense of kinship with each and every American. In leaving it, I do so with this prayer: May God's grace be with you in all the days ahead."

Bibliography

Doyle, James (1977). Not Above the Law: the battles of Watergate prosecutors Cox and Jaworski. New York: William Morrow and Company.

Hougan, Jim (1984). Watergate, Deep Throat and the CIA. New York: Random House, Inc.

Schudson, Michael (1992). Watergate in American memory: how we remember, forget, and reconstruct the past. New York: BasicBooks.

Holland, Max (2012). Leak: Why Mark Felt Became Deep Throat. Lawrence, KN: University

Press of Kansas.

White, Theodore Harold (1975). Breach of faith: the fall of Richard Nixon. New York: Atheneum Publishers.

Woodward, Bob and Bernstein, Carl (1974), All the President's Men

Woodward, Bob; Bernstein, Carl (2005). The Final Days. New York: Simon & Schuster.

Waldron, Lamar (2012). The Hidden History. Berkeley, California: Counterpoint publishers.

Printed in Great Britain
by Amazon.co.uk, Ltd.,
Marston Gate.